Wilhelm Heinrich Immanuel Bleek

On the Origin of Language

Wilhelm Heinrich Immanuel Bleek

On the Origin of Language

ISBN/EAN: 9783741180347

Manufactured in Europe, USA, Canada, Australia, Japa

Cover: Foto ©Andreas Hilbeck / pixelio.de

Manufactured and distributed by brebook publishing software
(www.brebook.com)

Wilhelm Heinrich Immanuel Bleek

On the Origin of Language

ON THE

ORIGIN OF LANGUAGE

o

BY

W. H. J. BLEEK,

DOCTOR OF PHILOSOPHY, CURATOR OF SIR G. GREY'S LIBRARY
IN CAPETOWN.

EDITED WITH A PREFACE BY

DR. ERNST HAECKEL,

PROFESSOR IN THE UNIVERSITY OF JENA.

TRANSLATED BY

THOMAS DAVIDSON.

NEW-YORK:

L. W. SCHMIDT, 24 BARCLAY STREET.

WEIMAR.   LONDON: PARIS:
H. BOEHLAU.   WILLIAMS & NORGATE.   C. REINWALD.

—

1869.

*" With every people, it is mainly its wealth of thought that assures its ascendency."—*JACOB GRIMM.

*" It is shown that human language retrogrades only in appearance and when viewed in detail; whereas, viewed in its entirety, it must ever appear progressing and augmenting its internal forces."—*Id.

EDITOR'S PREFACE.

In view of the separation which still ordinarily prevails between philology and natural science, it will cause certain persons some misgiving if a student of nature writes a few words of introduction to an essay on the science of language. Still, I was not unwilling to accede to the request of the publisher that I should accompany the following essay ON THE ORIGIN OF LANGUAGE with such an introduction. On the one hand, I am induced to do so by the close personal relations in which I stand to my cousin and friend, the author, who for the last thirteen years has resided in South Africa; on the other hand, by the close connection in which the subject of the essay stands to zoology, my professional department.

Wilhelm Bleek has for nearly twenty years given his attention to a comparative study of the South African languages, and has, since 1851, published a series of treatises on that subject:

De Nominum Generibus Linguarum Africæ australis, Copticæ, Semiticarum aliarumque sexualium. BONNÆ, 1851.

Ueber afrikanische Sprachverwandtschaft,—in den Monatsberichten der Berliner Gesellschaft für Erdkunde.

(*On the Relationship of the South African Languages*—in the Monthly Report of the Berlin Geographical Society) 1853.

On the Languages of Western and Southern Africa—in the
  Transactions of the Philological Society, 1855, No. 4.
The Languages of Mozambique.—Vocabularies, &c. LONDON,
  1856.
*The Library of H. E. Sir George Grey, K. C. B., Philo-
  logy*, Vol. 1, Africa. Vol. 2, Australia and Polynesia.
  CAPE TOWN, 1858, 1859.
*Reynard, the Fox, in South Africa. Hottentot Fables and
  Tales*, from Original Manuscripts. LONDON, 1864.
*A Comparative Grammar of South African Languages.
  Part 1, Phonology.* CAPE TOWN AND LONDON, 1862.

As is well known, the tribes of South Africa, the
Hottentots, the Bushmen, the Kaffirs, and others, branches
of the woolly-haired long-headed (dolichocephalic) family,
and usually looked upon as belonging to the negro stock,
have remained, down to the present day, at the lowest
stage of human development, and made the smallest
advance beyond the ape. This is true not only in respect
of their entire physical and moral characteristics, but also
in respect of their language. And surely this very fact
furnishes the author with a peculiar call and right to broach
the highly important fundamental question "On the
Origin of Language." It is only by a careful empirical
examination, and a thoughtful comparison of just those
original conditions of language, that the indispensable
inductive basis for the solution of that problem can be
obtained.

To attain this end, Wilhelm Bleek has spared neither
labor nor sacrifice. In order as far as possible to make
direct personal acquaintance with the languages and tribes
of South Africa, he in 1854 accompanied the expedition
for the exploration of the Benne (Jehadda), as scientific
commissioner of the English Government. Sickness,
however, compelled him to leave the expedition before it

ascended the Niger. Returning to England, he there met
Sir George Grey, the then recently appointed governor of
Cape Colony, and the first Bishop of Natal, the now celebrated Colenso. In the following year he accompanied the
latter to Natal, and during the year and a half that he spent
in this colony and in the country of the Zulus, he passed
many months in the hive-shaped huts of the natives.
(Petermann : Geographische Mittheilungen 1855, pp. 55,
145, 271, 361-369; 1856, pp. 362-373; 1857, pp. 99
and 266 ; 1856, p. 418.)

From this time, he labored in Cape Town, at first in
connection with Sir George Grey, who, with that lively
interest with which he is wont to further all scientific
efforts, took advantage of the numerous resources at his
command in order to bring together a collection of
materials as rich as possible for an accurate ethnological
and philological knowledge of the peoples and languages
of South Africa which have remained in such low conditions of culture. This collection forms part of the
library, extremely valuable also in other respects, (rich
particularly in old mss.), which Sir George Grey, on his
removal to New Zealand, in 1861, presented to Cape
Colony.

In his situation as librarian, Bleek soon found in Cape
Town other and manifold opportunities for becoming
more closely acquainted with those lower races of men,
who in every respect remind us of our animal ancestors,
and who, to the unprejudiced comparative student of ✗
nature, seem to manifest a closer connection with the
gorilla and chimpanzee of that region than with a Kant
or a Göthe.

Whilst Bleek's comparative studies in language were
thus positively favored by the immediate empirical
examination of those lowest stages of human linguistic

development, he enjoyed, through his protracted absence
from Europe, many negative advantages in addition.
Being removed from the unhealthy daily wrangling of
European schools of *savans*, and unbiassed by the influence
of prevailing authorities, he was able to rise freely to
the higher philosophical comparative stand-point which is
indispensable for the general treatment of so fundamental
a question. The reader will receive a vivid and manifold
impression from the widely extended view which that
stand-point affords for comparative anthropology, and
which the author to some extent developes in his preface.

The fact that this treatise, which was written a considerable time ago, is now published for the first time
may be regarded as a favorable circumstance in this
respect, that it will now find a much more receptive
public than it would have done at the time of its composition. Without any doubt it will derive advantage from
the enormous progress which has been made in scientific
acquirement generally, and particularly in the branch of
anthropology, since the appearance of Charles Darwin's
era-making book *On the Origin of Species.* The theory of
organic development which, as early as the beginning of
this century, was put forward by Lamarck and Göthe as
the only possible explanation of all biological phenomena,
and hence also of anthropological facts, has been placed
on a basis of mechanical causality by Darwin's theory of
selection. In zoölogy, which, in the first instance, is
more affected by this progress than all the other sciences,
Lamarck's and Darwin's theory of transmutation or
development forms already a basis which is indispensable.
In fact, it is now generally acknowledged as the basis of
zoölogy; for it is the only one that completely explains all
the general phenomena of zoölogy, while its opponents

have not been able to bring forward a really scientific explanation of a single one of these phenomena.

If, now, the doctrine of Lamarck, Göthe, and Darwin, that all animals are descended from one common type, or from a few such types, is really true, and it is beyond all doubt; and if, accordingly, this doctrine of transmutation is a great general law of induction, then we must set down as an inevitable consequence of it, as a deduction following necessarily from it, the conclusion that the human race also has arisen in a similar way, by the long and tedious path of organic development and transformation; that it likewise, through "natural selection in the struggle for existence," has gradually developed itself through different stages from low animal organisms, and immediately from a class of mammals resembling the apes. How this highly important conclusion has been established on a positive basis by all the general facts of zoölogy and anthropology, and especially by the history of the (embryological) development of man in particular, I have shown in detail in my *General Morphology of Organisms*, (Berlin, 1866, Vol. II, pp. cxii, 423, 432.)

This enormous progress in human knowledge, which lays the basis for a new and happy epoch in the history of the progressive development of the human spirit, owes its origin directly to the great progress made in the history of animal development, and the thoughtful appreciation which that subject has met with. But it is not merely zoölogy in its narrower sense, not merely comparative anatomy and physiology, that afford an immovable inductive basis for it. On the contrary, the results of geology, archæology, ethnology and geography, anthropology and linguistic inquiry, coming from all quarters unite in this one centre. They all verify and confirm that great, infinitely important law of development. The extraordi-

nary significance which has accrued from it to the com-
parative study of language has been demonstrated particu-
larly in the treatises of August Schleicher. (*The Darwinian
Theory and the Science of Language.* Weimar : 1863.
*On the Significance of Language for the Natural History of
Man.* Weimar : 1865.)

We may gladly welcome the following treatise by
Wilhelm Bleek as a further and highly important
contribution to the definite solution of this " question of
questions." As I have already stated in my lectures *On
the Origin and Genealogy of the Human Race* (Berlin, 1868),
the knowledge of the descent of man from a class of
lower animals will certainly hasten the progress of his
spiritual development and freedom in an extraordinary
degree. In this connection, the knowledge of the origin
of language plays a conspicuous part. In view of this,
Bleek's treatise may be warmly recommended not only to
natural investigators, but also to all persons of education
who take any interest in the great law of the progressive
development of humanity.

ERNST HAECKEL.

Jena, 1st July, 1868.

AUTHOR'S PREFACE.

THE rise of humanity is so recent an act in the history
of the development of mundane life, and the preparatory
stages which preceded the appearance of the human race
are so well known to us, that it can hardly be regarded
as anything extraordinary if we endeavor to form to ourselves some representation of the process which brought
us to that which distinguishes us from the animal world
and threw us into a higher path. Particularly at present,
when the tendency of all the more recent investigations
goes so much to strengthen the idea of progressive development in the production of the animal world, this
attempt seems merely a legitimate offspring of the time.
I must here, however, call attention to the fact that it
was written years ago, almost entirely as here printed.*
Jacob Grimm had then published one of his finest essays,
which was placed in a false light by its somewhat unsuit-
able title, *On the Origin of Language.* In connection
with this, Steinthal in a work, which must be reckoned
among the weakest productions of that able thinker, had
treated the same question, without, however, in any way
seizing its real solution. What the then youthful, though
not untrained, student of language required was to make

* It formed part of a work which competed in 1853 for the Volney
prize. The publication has hitherto been prevented by the author's
many years' absence from Europe.

himself clear regarding that which his masters did not explain to him.

I am not aware that any attempt has ever been made to answer the question in this manner—the only one, it seems to me, which is scientifically possible.

Many readers of this explanation, in order to gain a clearer idea of the matter, will perhaps, and with good reason, ask in what period of time the occurrences here described are to be placed. This question, nevertheless, does not in any way essentially affect the results of our inquiry : but yet I see no reason why what has hitherto been obtained in the way of general and all-embracing results from our examination of the career of linguistic development should not be summed up in a few words.

It would carry us too far were we to state the manner in which the minuter details are worked out. For this reason, I have the less right to demand that our estimate should be accepted without further question. Yet I think we make a very moderate calculation when we place the epoch at which man became man a hundred thousand years before our usual reckoning. This is an estimate which years ago seemed to force itself upon me by the mere consideration of the space of time necessary for the formation of those differences of development manifested in what are called the old-world languages. It may, however, well be that, instead of one hundred thousand years, several, yea, many hundred thousand years, belong to the history of humanity.

Still, the solution of this question does not lie in the region of philology, but in that of palæontology. And in in this respect, it is a real pleasure to observe with what approximative certainty important results have been arrived at already, when only a few districts of country have been geologically examined with any thoroughness.

When I reflect how, something like twelve years ago, when one evening, in the course of conversation with one of the most prominent geologists of our time, I touched upon this subject, he referred the discussion of the question respecting the age of the human race, and the epoch as well as the scene of his first appearance, to much later stages of geological research, and regarded it as hardly at present a possible subject of investigation—when, I say, I make this reflection, the appearance of Sir Charles Lyell's work *On the Antiquity of Man* shows me with what gigantic strides European science has progressed. To us here in the Southern hemisphere, so far removed from the bustle of the European learned world, this seems all the clearer that frequently only the results, without the daily progress, of the researches of our northern friends are accessible to us. That, nevertheless, we exert ourselves to follow with lively interest, at least in its salient points, the course of these investigations, even this attempt may serve to show in some small degree to our friends at home.

I should like here to call attention to the fact that hitherto no sufficient inquiry seems to have been instituted into how far the lower animals are endowed with language. So far as I can make out at present, that which they possess analogous to language occupies almost the same position as printing from blocks does as compared with printing from moveable types. If, for example, we must really refuse to acknowledge that the Chinese are in possession of the art of printing (as we understand it in Europe), we cannot say that the lower animals possess language in the real sense of the term—least of all, articulate language. But as there is only a step from printing with blocks to printing with types, so in those means of expression which the animals use to communicate their feelings we find the elements out of which, under favorable circumstances (which rendered the division of speech into articulate elements possible), it was possible for human language to arise.

This view, that the insight which is possible for humanity had its origin in the unintelligence of the lower animals, is to me not at all a degrading one, but seems in the highest degree elevating and hope-inspiring. For the advance which we have already made, and the comparison of what we have attained with what we have left behind, cannot but inspire us with the deepest hopefulness in regard to the attainments which our race may yet possibly make. We must not indeed in any manner undervalue those large acquisitions which we have made through the possession of articulate speech, nor the penetrating character of the distinction which this establishes between us and the lower animals.

In discussing the question as to the position which man ought to occupy in a scientific classification of organic beings, it seems to me that one important point has been too frequently overlooked, viz: the fact that, although the differences in structure between the individual man and those species of animals that are most closely related to him are hardly so great as those that exist between these and the lower apes, yet the individual man is only an inseparable part of the entire human race, inasmuch as he cannot continue to exist as a man in anything like complete isolation. The race itself must be looked upon as an individual organism, in every respect enormously grander than any other organism with which we are acquainted. In this very fact, that the lower animals can not through articulate speech make the acquisitions of the individual or of the generation the common property of the race, lies the ground of the other fact that all progress of the race as such, and hence all actual united and therefore imper-

ishable and immortal life for the race is in their case
impossible. The endowment of speech is the cement that
binds together all the parts of the gigantic organism of
humanity, and the expressions of this endowment bear a
certain analogy to the circulation of the blood in the
animal body. The individual man holds merely the same
relation to the real unit of entire humanity as a single
cell holds to the whole of a great organic being, whether
it be a unit in the animal or in the vegetable world. But,
as the single elements of an organic being are correctly
appreciated physiologically only when viewed in connection with the whole of the particular organism to which
it belongs; so, also, we arrive at a true understanding of
what the individual man is, not so much by a comparison
of his physical constitution with that of the animals that
are most closely related to him, as by a correct comprehension of his relation to the great whole whereof he forms
but an infinitesimal part. And as the nature of inorganic
substances alters entirely when they become components
of an organic being; so, also, and in a much higher degree,
are the powers and capabilities of the animals affected,
when (and to the extent that) the body of the individual
man is penetrated by the spiritual power conditioned
by his position in the whole of the great organism of
humanity.

We give the name of spirit to the eternal and imper-
ishable (element) in the relation of man to humanity, the
element which penetrates the whole organism with its
life-giving properties and renders it capable of a larger
unity and a progressively higher development,—which
penetrates each particular part, yea, each particular
particle, to a greater or less extent. According to his
participation in this vital element of the whole is determined the significance of the individual man—whether

in an animal sort of way he appropriates the attainments
which have descended to him, or uses his efforts to carry
these forward to higher developments. To realize in
himself the internal and external harmony of his race in
some way or another, and to further the proper relations
of the different parts to each other in their connection as
limbs and larger divisions of the entire organism, (for
example, of the bonds of family, state and nation, held
together by ties of kinship, community of laws, or simi-
larity of language,) these are the highest aims of human
existence visible to him—aims that must of themselves
incite him to noble deeds and virtuous actions. In the
accomplishment of these tasks lies the highest happiness
that appears to be accorded to our race—a happiness
accessible to every individual of it in his own particular
way.

And it appears to me that the attainment of such
happiness is very much facilitated when in this manner
the highest tasks of man are shown to be those which are
easiest in accordance with the natural view of his constitution. For, as soon as we have clearly seen that
individual life and action are in reality only small fragments
of the great everlasting life of humanity, and that it is
only in and through participation in it that the individual
man actually lives—and, we may hope, lives forever—
the realization of the universal best appears no longer as
a duty difficult to fulfil, but as a necessity of our nature,
which we shall be the less able to resist the more we
comprehend the true nature of things. And in truth it
is the feeling of such a relation that is the life-spring of
all good and noble efforts. Neither the fear of everlasting
damnation, nor the hope of individual bliss, are really of
sufficient strength, as true saving ideas, to raise men to a
higher existence ; and this apart from the fact that each of

these two fundamental doctrines of the vulgar dogmatism in reality makes a merely refined selfishness the lever of its ethics.

Whether, and in how far, a continuance of the identity of the individual beyond the grave is possible is a question with which our ethics at present have nothing to do; and it is a mere paltry ethical view which supposes that it must support itself upon such ideas, lying beyond our comprehension. Even granted (and I do not mean either to affirm or deny it) that such a continuance of life for the individual man were proved; in any case, the mode and manner of it are altogether uncertain, and for that reason alone, if for no other, it cannot form a sure and solid foundation (which is indispensable to ethics as to every other edifice) for our moral convictions.

It must, however, here be distinctly stated that this idea of what is called personal immortality is not specifically a Christian one, or one that owes its origin to the sacred writings of the Jews or Christians.

Ancestor-worship, a form of religion which must be reckoned among the most ancient, is entirely based upon this view. However, when the personification of natural phenomena, having its origin in the sexual form of language, filled the sky with gods, this idea of the personal prolonged existence of man after death was in some measure thrown into the back-ground; notwithstanding that in hero-worship, which is so frequently mixed up with this form of religion, the ancient ancestor-worship is still represented in greater or less degree.

That modern theology, however, has grown upon the ground and soil of a mythology which arose out of the original personification and consequent worship of celestial phenomena, is demonstrated in the most striking manner by the mere use of the word heaven as the abode

of the spirit-world. In the old ancestor-worship, on the
contrary, the abode of the spirits is under the earth, and
paradise, as well as the residence of the gods (or of what
appears here analogous to the gods), lies in a sort of cave.
Heaven, on the contrary, does not appear to the ancestor-
worshippers to have any religious or otherwise elevating
significance.

The nations among which we find this ancestor-worship
still prevailing are chiefly those which speak prefix-
pronominal languages, as the Kaffirs and Negro tribes of
tropical Africa and their oceanic relatives as far as New
Zealand and the Sandwich Islands.

That a person who during his life-time has exercised a
greater or less influence upon the fortunes of his family,
tribe, or nation, should be cut off by death from such
expression of power, seems to people at a certain stage of
thought almost impossible, particularly in cases in which
many persons have been wont to look up to him with
reverence. The head of the tribe, for example, in states
of civilization in which polygamy prevails, (and almost
all peoples addicted to ancestor-worship and speaking
prefix-pronominal languages are polygamists), counts his
children by dozens and his grand-children by hundreds,
while the number of *protégés* and other subjects to whom
in like manner he stands as rightful father is usually
much greater still. For all these, his word is life and
death. Their whole existence seems to depend on him.
They know that it is well with them, and that they can
prosper, only when he is favorably disposed toward them.
To conciliate him when he is angry, or to win his favor
when any thing is desired of him, or, to express gratitude
for favors already received, gifts are brought to him of
such kinds as are supposed likely to be most acceptable to
him. How then is it possible that such a lofty being

should be mortal, and in and through death should thus
entirely lose the power that guides his tribe! Even
yet, faith firmly maintains, the deceased has the welfare
of his beloved children at heart; even yet, he exercises
a considerable influence upon their fortunes, and can,
according as he wishes, make the individual happy or
unhappy. It is to his favor that they still owe all good,
and their fortunes darken before his wrath. Moreover,
he can still be propitiated by gifts and sacrifices, flattered
with praises, and approached with entreaties.

How this is the true origin of all divine worship, and
even of the modern theological doctrine of atonement,
will become manifest as we follow the history of the
development of the religious intuition.

Ancestor-worship, in the form above stated (and this is
evidently its original form), seems very natural. Nevertheless, in the different modes of its development (as such,
and through the consequent belief in the continued corpo-
real life of the deceased), it has often led to the strangest
results. As for example, when, according to the New
Zealanders, the most malevolent spirits are the souls of
children that have died before their birth. And what
strange pictures and even humorous traits would a history
of belief in ghosts bring to light, even if it were confined
to European soil! It does appear to us astonishing
when we hear that Mongolian peoples, and even the
ancient Persians, as soon as those of the deceased who had
fallen a prey to an early death, had in their graves reached
a marriageable age, married them to each other or even
to living persons, and celebrated such marriage feasts
with great solemnity. And yet how many a sentimental
girl's heart, in our most cultivated circles, has lived on
the thought that there must exist a heart corresponding
to hers, with which, either here below or in the world

3

beyond, here will be united in indissoluble union! Those ruder peoples have merely endeavored to carry out this thought in the most sensuous manner.

The ancestor-worshipper's gods (if we may call the objects of his worship gods) appear to him most frequently in dreams, thus reveal their will to him, and even announce future events accurately, when the dream-spirits (which, therefore, are called in Zulu *a Ma-tongo* 6, plural of *i-Tongo* 5, a dream-spirit,) are well disposed to the dreamer. If, on the contrary, they are angry with him, they flutter round and delude him with deceptive promises, whose non-fulfilment accordingly announces the wrath of the dream-spirits. In order to conciliate them, sacrifices must then be offered, or purifications instituted for that purpose.*

This is the beginning of an ethical intuition, wherein each of our actions and thoughts is viewed in its relation to an invisible object grasped merely by the imagination. And at this period of the development of religious life, men begin to accustom themselves more or less to see, in fortunes and events, the work of the passions of spirits having volition like men, and yet not appearing in human

---

* On the occasion of a visit to the court of *Mpánde*, king of the Zulus, I one day saw among the crowd of courtiers who petitioned me for gifts several of the wives of one of the chief Zulu princes. The youngest of these petitioned me for one particular thing, a kind of ornament that is worn in the country of the Zulus. I offered her another present, and one which, I presume, was as valuable in her eyes. However, she persisted in her original request, stating as her reason for so doing that she had dreamt that I would give her the thing which she then asked for. Unfortunately I adhered inexorably to my refusal—and in fact I should soon have been stripped of all my property, if I had once begun to make presents to the Zulus in accordance with their dreams. The young lady went away mourning, and complaining that the dream-spirit had deceived her, and that she should now have to purify herself before him.

form. To render these favorably disposed, or when they are angry, to conciliate them, is of course the duty and desire of the faithful ancestor-worshipper.

This belief is strengthened not only by dream visions, but also by apparitions during the day of the spirits of the deceased, chiefly in the form of animals—for example, serpents, as they most frequently appear among the Zulus.

However, there is certainly here no personification of the animal, such as we find in the fable-world of our earliest literature. The imagination of the ancestor-worshipper does not for the most part go even so far as to endow the animals with human speech, but merely makes them perform, with animal dumbness, actions which are within the limits of the capacity of animals, but which, in the individual animals, into which the souls of deceased persons have passed, are regarded as proceeding from these souls. The serpent *i-Îozi* 5 (or ancestor-ghost) among the Zulus, slinks into the most remote corner, in order to feed upon the pieces of flesh that are there hung up as offerings, or it enters into combat with other serpents, which represent *aMa-Îozi* 6, of such deceased-persons as the spirit represented by the first serpent was hostile to during life.

The spirit-world of pure ancestor-worship is distinguished by this characteristic, that the beings endowed with human volition (which are either altogether invisible, or visible only as animals, or in some other non-human form) have always been actual human beings. Of a personification of the animal world (such as we find in our fables) or even of other things (as we find chiefly in our mythology) this primeval prosaic view as yet knows nothing.

Such a poetic flight of imagination takes place contemporaneously with and in consequence of a development of the form of language—a development which, to judge from its results, must certainly be regarded as one of the most important. But, to make this plain, I must go a little farther into detail.

For the majority of us (we might without exaggeration say, for nine thousand nine hundred and ninety-nine in every ten thousand) who during our whole lives employ only sexual languages,* the distinction of the gender of nouns according to sex seems a matter of course—in fact, almost a natural thing. Many persons (for example, to name only one of the most distinguished names, Grimm, in his German Grammar, that giant work of profound investigation) have tried to recognize in the kind of distinction which we make between the genders, a profound, delicately excogitated view of the nature of things.

It is only the practical sense of the English, who, as a matter of fact, have themselves altered and brought into almost complete accordance with reason, the original distinction of gender, that asks with astonishment why in the world, in German, for example, the bottle (*die Flasche*) is apparently a lady, and the table (*der Tisch*) a gentleman.

The history of the development of language, however, shows us that the distinction which is made in our languages between the genders of nouns does not rest upon any intentional division of the ideas expressed, but upon the fact that the nouns were originally capable of being replaced by their most essential components; which, however, do not now occur as separate words—that is to say, unless they were used in this manner as pronouns.

* For almost all European languages, as well as all the rest of the Aryan ones (also the Semitic languages, and even the Egyptian), in fact almost all civilized languages belong to the sexual family of languages.

The nouns which in this way are replaced by their same pronouns then form a class, the extent and character of which depends at first on the more or less extensive use of the noun-factor which serves to replace the nouns.*

Thus in the prefix-pronominal languages we find a large number of classes of nouns (in some as many as eighteen) or genders whereof not one has any relation to the distinction of sex. In these languages, the very words for man and woman are not in different classes, because they are not formed with different derivative syllables. The names of human beings, on the contrary, are in the singular, usually put in the same class, with a corresponding plural class.

This setting apart of beings endowed with speech as a particular grammatical class, appears to have led to the specific prominence lent to it, which must be regarded as the ground of ancestor-worship, and which even forms the basis of the religion of nearly all the peoples who speak prefix-pronominal languages.

On the other hand, in those suffix-pronominal languages which we designate as belonging to the sexual family, no common class for human beings was formed in this manner; but as the words for man and woman were formed with different derivative syllables, they were also replaced by different pronouns, and thus found their way into different classes or genders. That those classes of nouns, for example, in which the words for man, and at the same time, the majority of the words expressing male beings, occurred, should thereby have impressed upon them the character of the masculine gender, was entirely natural. When the use of a pronoun which, with words designating human beings, implied a difference of gender,

* I must here refer my readers to the second part of my Comparative Grammar on the South-African languages, now in the press.

extended itself to inanimate objects, this produced at
once a distinction among them, on the analogy of the
distinction of sex, having application to persons.

But now, to view things as if they stood to each other
in the relation of man and woman, and so were affected
by the most intense and engrossing passions, was to
endow them with humanity in the highest degree, and
thus to lend them an interest of peculiar importance, such
as they could not in and for themselves have been enabled
in any other way to claim from persons ignorant of their
internal connection, and the power which the knowledge
of them imparts to man. That which appears to us as
guided by a power of volition analogous to our own, and
in which we suppose the existence of passions and appetites of a human character, must interest us from the
very first, and thereby it comes immediately, in a mythical
way, into a peculiar relation to us. Thousands of exam-
ples might be adduced to illustrate this, and to make us
feel how much a personification of inanimate things, or
the endowing of impersonal existences with human attributes, sharpens our powers of observation and spurs us
on to a better comprehension of the actual relations
of things.

Is it, then, a mere accident that nearly all the nations
which have made any progress in scientific acquirement
speak sexual languages?* Certainly, the sexual class
includes the languages of the Egyptians, Babylonians,
Hebrews, Phœnicians, Arabs, ancient Hindoos, Medes,

* How far, in this respect, Japanese and Chinese science forms an
exception, I do not venture to say; particularly as it is not yet
certain whether the Chinese language must not be regarded as
having belonged, at least originally, to the sexual class of languages.
Many indications seem to show that, along with other formal elements, the grammatical genders of the nouns were lost.

Greeks and Romans, German, and all the peoples whose
languages are akin to these.

On the other hand, among the mass of nations speaking
prefix-pronominal languages, many of which form extensive political unions, there is not one that has added any
noteworthy contribution to scientific knowledge; and
not a single individual who could be called great as
thinker, inventor, or poet has risen among them. This
fact is, doubtless, the result of an organic defect, the
ground of which lies in the lack of any power of seizing
poetically the constitution of things. The grammatical
form of their languages does not allow their imagination
that higher flight which the form of the sexual languages
irresistibly imparts to the movement of the thought of
those that speak them.

This enables us to see why the mode of speech, and
hence also the mode of thought, prevalent among peoples
who speak prefix-pronominal languages is strikingly
practical and prosaic. Of poetry, as well as of science,
mythology, and philosophy, there is hardly even a trace
among them.

The form of a sexual language, by exciting in us sym-
pathies for that which is not united to us by a common
humanity, leads in the first instance to the endowment of
animals with human attributes, and in this way gives
occasion for the invention of fables. Even at the lowest
stage of national development, we find the language of the
Hottentots possessing a fable literature, for the counter-
part of which we should look in vain in the literatures of
the prefix-pronominal languages.

Still, the endowment of animals with human attributes,
and the personification of impersonal things, do not necessarily lead to the adoration of these objects. Only when
objects are personified whose power, when they are

viewed as endowed with human life, evidently far exceeds the power of the individual man, does the feeling of great superiority make itself valid—a feeling which, in and by itself, inclines the mind to reverent consideration.

At the lowest stage of culture which we find among peoples of sexual speech, among the Hottentots, religious reverence of this kind for the heavenly bodies prevails to such a small extent, simply because the knowledge of the significance of their movements necessary for a worshipful apprehension is as yet so slightly developed. Still we find the beginning of a mythological apprehension of them even among that people. But it is plain from the mode and manner in which, in all the myths (even in the most significant of all, the one relating to the origin of death), the sun and moon coöperate with animals, that myth and fable are here still undistinguished.

Among the Hottentots, the phases of the moon seem principally to attract attention. The gradual increase and decrease of the appearance of this heavenly body seems to give it the semblance of a being that waxes and again wanes, and one which readily lends itself to personification. It is therefore not improbable that the worship of the moon was the earliest phase of star-worship. In regard to the Hottentots, Kolb, for the most part a trustworthy informant, tells us that they pay divine worship to the moon. The moon (||khăp*) is among them, as well as in the Old-Germanic languages, masculine, and the sun (*soris*) feminine.

The Hottentot fables include myths relating to the sun even; and although its unchanging appearance is not so likely to give occasion for personification as the more

---

* || Is the lateral click, *kh* a guttural consonant, and ⁻ indicates the nasal pronunciation.

inconstant moon, it has been, nevertheless, obliged to
follow closely the personification of the latter.*

A further step was taken in passing from the worship
of the moon and the sun to a general star-worship. As
soon as this point was arrived at, there followed, on the
one hand, a development of mythological thought, whose
last offshoot is our theology, and, on the other, arose
astrology, and its older surviving sister, astronomy.
But it was through the latter that the veil of mist, in
which mythology and theology had wrapped our whole
existence, was at last lifted.

In any case, this poetical view was a most important
transition stage in the ascent towards true scientific knowledge. It does seem as if it had been necessary that
the heavenly bodies should appear engaged in an eternal
dance, and as actively influencing the life of the individual
man; moreover, as if it had been necessary that the
elements should be conceived as moved by spirits, and
therefore the universe as guided by beings endowed with

* The worship of the sun and the moon that prevails among many
American tribes is capable of being explained in two ways. Either
the civilization of these peoples is traceable to that of the sexual
nations, and so was probably introduced among them from Asia,
or else the languages of all, or at least some, of these American
culture-nations belonged originally to the sexual family of languages.
If the latter is the case, we may assume with certainty that traces of
this original kinship will be discovered on sufficiently accurate examination. That the prefix-pronominal family sent off shoots across to
America seems to me beyond question, although the language in
which, as I believe, I have found traces of this family (the language
of the Dacotahs), stands to it perhaps only in the same sort of relation
as English stands to the Romance languages. But as the present
condition of English affords evidence of the earlier existence of
Norman-French in England, so certain distinct marks in the Dacotah
language appear to show that it must have been for a long-time under
the influence of prefix-pronominal languages.

4

human volition, and therefore subject to human limita
tions, in order that our interest in the existence of things
which appear as standing in such kinship to us, and hence
in closer relation, might excite us to a more profound
study of the world of phenomena, and that thus we might
approach, in some small degree, a knowledge of the final
ground of all existence, and, to a considerable extent, an
understanding of the mutual relations of the objects that
lie nearest to us.

As soon, then, as the imagination, incited by the form
of language, had endowed either the heavenly bodies, or
any other objects or abstractions that appear to the
individual man as accompanied with gigantic power, with
human attributes, the result could hardly fail to be that
the worship, which had hitherto been paid to the spirits
of the great departed, should be transferred to these new
and grand personages who were likewise *not* visible to the
eye in human shape. All the changes that were observed
in them were naturally looked upon as tokens of their
caprice, as marks of their favorable or unfavorable disposition.

Thus, the upward gaze of adoration turned gradually
from the spirits of the dead to the supposed spirits of
nature—and this all the more strongly as increased insight
disclosed the significance of the forces of nature. To win
the favor of these sublime personages, and to avert their
wrath, now became, of necessity, the chief motive of
religious life.

It is not possible, within the limits of a mere preface
to pursue the forms of the so-called religious idea—or, to
speak more correctly, the mythological conception of the
nature of the deity—through all its manifold stages and
ramifications. In this relation, we will simply remark
that, in general, higher ethical ideas go along with a deeper

apprehension of the nature of the deity, and that, on the
other hand, the manner of this apprehension depends
essentially upon the character of the cognizer, and
the degree in which he has arrived at a scientific cognition.

But the grand turning-point on which the mythological
apprehension splits is marked by the rise of the idea of
the necessity of atonement. For, at bottom, all so-called
religious modes of thought based upon the idea that one
or more invisible personages have to be conciliated are
essentially of the same character. But there is no abso-
lute, though relatively there is a very considerable, difference between the feeling of the Kaffir who pleads with
his forefathers to forgive him his misdeeds, and the contri-
tion of a penitent sinner who is involved in the notions of
popular theology. In both, the mythological anthropo-
morphical conception of the nature of God, as a being who
must be appeased or conciliated like a human being, is
the main lever of the consciousness of dependence and of
the religious attitude.

It is only when man has come to recognize it as an
impossibility that a being similar to man should be the
final ground of all existence, and to confess with reverent
modesty his ignorance of the nature of the primal ground
of things, that he learns to see what a trivial view he has,
in any case, of the Being that appears to him worthy of
the highest adoration, if he supposes that, with his limited
knowledge, he can in any way grasp the nature of Deity
and understand His plans and ideas. But this is just
what is done by all theology, which, therefore, appears to
us essentially a piece of presumption—a presumption,
however, of which most theologians are unaware. In the
same way, the astrologers had seldom even the slightest
notion to what extent they cut the thread of scientific

inquiry when they supposed they had already discovered the relation in which the star-world stands to us.

We do not mean by this to affirm that the efforts of all so-called theologians have been of no service to science. On the contrary, as the actual studies and observations of the astrologers frequently benefited astronomy, so many of the works of so-called theologians maintain their position as valuable and lasting contributions to science. In this relation, it is a satisfactory feeling to know that every honest and earnest endeavor after truth, however much one may be groping in the dark as regards method and fundamental view, will one day produce its fruit. In fact, it is theology itself, and chiefly the philosophy that has grown out of it (by dealing seriously with its problem, and carrying the theological principles to their consequences), that makes manifest its untenability and its unsatisfactory character. It can do this, however, only when it views with the sharpness of scientific method the image of the past, and does not reconcile itself with it in a merely poetical way.

If, on the one side, we thus endeavor to strip off theological presumption as a heathen element that has descended to us from the mythological stage, on the other, the true religious feeling, as arising from the fulness of self-consciousness, must gain in intensity in proportion to the spiritual development of humanity as such. It increases in strength chiefly through and along with that deeper insight into the essence of things which is furthered by greater scientific clearness. If, on the one hand, the coloring of theological pre-suppositions contributes only to the weakening of the religious sense, on the other, the humble confession of the insufficiency of all theological definitions is the fundamental premise of a pure religious disposition.

Before I close this preface, I wish to remark that, in this treatise, undertaken as it is from the philological stand-point, the certainly undeniable fact of the immediate connection of the faculty of language in man with the peculiar constitution of his brain has not been taken into consideration. It may be that, when the progress of physiology shall have placed this point in a clearer light, it will enable us to make further contributions to the history of the origin of language. I may state however, as a passing remark, that I see no reason why the development and refinement of the material of the brain, and the consequent faculty of speech and higher power of thought, should not be regarded as the results of continued energetic effort on the part of more original brain-forms. How much the constitution of the brain depends upon its greater or less activity is generally well known. This is what has given occasion to the higher cerebral activity which has led to the development of those distinctive characteristics of the human brain. How the development-processes of lower faculties and tendencies have produced a new force, by which, as a natural consequence, the brain has been affected in a quite peculiar way, is the question here attempted to be investigated.

W. H. I. BLEEK.

Cape Town, May 30, 1867

ON THE

ORIGIN OF LANGUAGE

AS A FIRST CHAPTER IN A

HISTORY OF THE DEVELOPMENT
OF HUMANITY.

Citius emergit veritas ex errore quam ex confusione.

THE ORIGIN OF LANGUAGE.

We move upon a giddy height when we attempt to know the direction of the world's development. And yet the contemplation of the successive phases of the Universe which our eye has hitherto been able to seize leads naturally to further conclusions ir reference to the whole course of development, whereof all that we have hitherto been able to learn forms but a very small part.

The direction of the world's development seems to have for its aim the production of a being more and more capable of volition, because continually advancing in power and self-consciousness. It is on purpose that I abstain from using the word *plan* in this connection. For I believe that a plan always implies a purpose, and a purpose is only a determinate product of will—that is to say, of a purely human function. As soon as it is clearly understood that an act of volition can belong only to a being whose knowledge is limited, and who, on all occasions, makes an arbitrary choice between two things with limited insight, it is no longer possible to speak of the plan or purpose of the world's evolution. Since it is manifestly beyond our powers of comprehension to understand the nature of the last ground of all existence, it is certainly a piece of presumption on our part to ascribe to it a sublimated human essence. Fichte was right in saying that God ought not to be thought in connection with

the world of sense, or, indeed, at all; and this for the
simple reason that it is impossible so to think Him.

If, therefore, it appears impossible for us, from the nature
of our understanding, to grasp anything beyond the laws
according to which the elements involuntarily act upon
each other, we can speak no longer of the purpose, but
only of the result of the process of the world's evolution; we must seek to recognize in it, not a plan, but a
course of development.

It is only when an efficient power begins self-consciously
to distinguish itself from its objects, and determines its
own direction according to choice, that systematic action
and subordination to determinate ends begin.[*]

Now that such a being, having its basis in self-consciousness, should be inclined to look, in other activi-
ties, which come under its notice, for a constitution similar to its own, is easily conceivable. But in the same

* Of course I do not here mean to deny the possibility (personally
I have a firm belief in the actuality), but merely the conceivability
of a higher working, analogous to our directive activity. But it is
extremely necessary to guard oneself against the insinuation of the
prevalent anthropomorphism, which conceives the deity in a fashion
homologous with our own nature. One, indeed, is sorry to see a man
like L. Agassiz, who observes so finely and seizes so acutely, again
falling into this mistake, notwithstanding that in other connections he
clearly sees the unsatisfactory character of this mode of adducing
proof, which prevails notably in *The Bridgewater Treatises*, (*On
Classification*, 1859, p. 11.) The fact that his spirited discussions
will not fail to accomplish the beneficent purpose of putting a stop
to the loose employment of a scientific terminology is due, not so
much to the fundamental thought which they pre-suppose, as to the
genial eye of their author, who, in spite of his dogmatic bias, could
not help recognizing the truth in almost all individual cases. It is
true that a greater degree of elasticity must be imparted to the
intermediate sections of a system, in order to make it comprehend
rightly, and without forcing, the results of actual observations, and to
prevent it from degenerating into mere scheme-making.

manner as the progress of knowledge has caused us to give over regarding the elements, the heavenly bodies, the passions and appetites, as beings endowed with human power of volition, clear insight forbids us to represent the Universe as moved by a power analogous to the human. The ground of all existence cannot be measured in its infinity by finite magnitudes. And for the reason that it is less susceptible of representation than anything else, it is less suited than anything else for being a starting-point of investigation. It is the final goal of all knowledge, which, in proportion as it progresses, comes nearer the intuition of it. Whether this approximation will ever be able to ascend beyond a mere guess, we hold to be more than doubtful.

Although we must be on our guard against all *a priori* constructions, and against the insinuation of all false principles of explanation, still the only aim of our science must ever be to discover how it has happened that such a being, endowed with self-consciousness and power of volition has developed itself; by what process it arrived at those differences of culture which we find existing among different nations and individuals, and what is likely, from the peculiarity of its constitution, and from what we know to be the conditions of its evolution and that of the Universe generally, to be the end of it. Of these three problems the last belongs more properly to the sphere of speculation than to that of scientific knowledge. But in proportion as we arrive at certain results in the other two, the greater will be the amount of truth imparted to the conclusions based upon them in regard to our future.

The discovery of the mode in which man came into existence is the aim of what are called the natural sciences, whereas, the investigation of the process of human

development is the task of philology or history, these
terms being used as identical and with a much more
general signification than that in which they are usually
employed. These two disciplines, philology and physics,
are distinguished most clearly, as regards their different
aims, by the mode of observation peculiar to each.*

As the separation between the two disciplines takes
place naturally, the investigations and results of the one
need not therefore remain foreign to the other. They
mutually complement each other, and it is only when the
two are combined that they form science ; neither by itself
can be called a science ; each is only a scientific discipline.
Instead, therefore, of the misleading term, Natural
Science, we prefer Natural Research, and range the latter
alongside Philology or Historical Research. For although
the activity of the investigator of nature is to be distinguished, in this way, from that of the philologist or
student of history, still we do not see that we are justified
in holding these two separate, especially if we take the
concept of philology in a more general, and that of
historical research in a more extended sense, so that the
former shall not confine itself to a few peoples, and the

* Max Müller, in his spirited *Lectures on the Science of Language*
(London, 1861) seems to me inconsequent in assigning the study of
language to the domain of the natural sciences. Students of
language will always of necessity be philologists, and will derive no
more profit from physics than one scientific discipline always derives
from another. It is indeed true that at bottom science is one ; but
practically (*i. e.* as regards methods and means of investigation), as
well as theoretically (*i. e.* as regards the object of investigation)
there is a clear enough distinction between the two disciplines.
The science of language stands in closer relation to physics
than any other branch of philology does, inasmuch as by it the
original skeleton of the entire history of human development is laid
bare.

latter shall include not merely political development, but
all human evolution generally.

To return, however, to the relation between natural
research and philology (for we prefer this term to historical research); on one side our knowledge of the
constitution of things depends entirely upon the extent
to which we have arrived at clearness in regard to the
nature of our own power, and the range of human
knowledge. True knowledge is arrived at only when we
know how we know, that is, when we have comprehended our own nature. This problem, which philology
must endeavor to solve by an investigation of the course
of human development, is therefore of the highest
importance at the same time for natural research.

But in order to arrive at this insight into the constitution of human nature, it is not enough to take into
consideration merely the course which its development
has run, and the various conditions in which we observe
it to have resulted. No, the history of human development is merely a part of the history of the development
of the universe, and can be comprehended only in connection therewith. The essential nature of the course
of human development can become clear to us only when
we endeavor thus to discover the origin of our race, and
to arrive at the characteristics which distinguish it and
mark it out.

If then the two disciplines have the same object, if the
highest problem of natural research is that of the formation
of human nature, and the sole problem of philology is to
pursue still farther its various development; it is clear
that a one-sided devotion to either, inasmuch as at bottom
they aim at the same mark, though in different ways, can
lead only to error. Each has to learn, not only from the
results, but also from the methods of the other.

But how far distant is still the time when this thought shall be realized in the harmonious fusion of the two disciplines! How long will it be before philology shall have risen to that height on which the disciplines of natural research at present stand and from which they justly claim the favor of the moment!

But it cannot do this—it cannot assert its right to a place among real scientific disciplines, until it is studied purely for its own sake, without any reference to æsthetic or educational aims, although the method in which it is usually conducted in Germany at present gives small promise of ever allowing even these to be reached.* This method (in which, notwithstanding, a considerable progress has become apparent, inasmuch as an exact and methodical treatment is the necessary condition of all real scientific knowledge) has, on the other hand, led again to one-sidedness in this way, that in theory, and still more in practice, the most accurate possible restoration of the text of ancient authors has been set forth as the aim of philology. "Sufficiently has the past been investigated by us without any reference to the universally human in it," says Bunsen in his memorable preface to the German edition of *Hippolytus.*

Philology must not only become more and more conscious of its great aim—the discovery of the process of human development, of the position which we hold in it, and the manner in which our efforts can be made to contribute to its advancement; but with this view, it must

* I beg leave to remark that, since this was written, the author's long residence in Africa has withdrawn him from immediate observation of the progress of philology in Germany during the last twelve years, so that it is possible that what was a correct statement in respect to this then, is now no longer applicable. *Remark by Dr. Haeckel.*

enter upon a series of hitherto almost untrodden paths; it must renounce prejudices, which, though long since overcome in the other disciplines, still hold it back. How far would botany, for example, have progressed, if the study of it had been confined to the plants useful for the kitchen and the drug-store, or to those which please the sense of sight or smell? And in like manner how would it be with chemistry, if the properties of only those substances which are medicinally or commercially important had been deemed worthy of investigation?

Only when every peculiarly developed member of humanity is considered worthy of attention, and investigation turns with as much zeal to the conditions of those peoples which have stopt short at the lowest phases of development, as to those of the most cultured nations—which it can properly understand and comprehend only by a comparison with those less developed ones—only then may we speak of a universal philology in the true sense of the term, and place it on an equal footing alongside natural research. Only when in this way an inexhaustible fund of new ideas, materially affecting our view of the world, has been secured, has it a right to look for a fresh awakening of the nation's sympathy in its behalf—a sympathy, however, which will be accorded to it in far larger measure than it now is to natural research. For it speaks to man of man; and this after all is the most important subject of contemplation, the one which must most concern man.

Universal philology does not confine its efforts simply to pursuing the development and growth of each particular race, and to connecting together such results as may be obtained touching the progress of the method of human development universally. No, its task is one that goes much deeper. It must endeavor earnestly to obtain a picture of the whole course of human development; must examine how the conditions of the individual nations, investigation of which is the task of special branches of philological study, arose out of a former undistinguished existence, of which no monuments or written records remain to us, and attained their present distinct and variform character. A solution of this problem is of course possible only when the conditions of different nations have been shown to have arisen out of *one* and the same original condition. A careful comparison must then show what each individual nation has preserved from the original source, and what it owes to later culture, attained whether by native power or through foreign influence. The sum of the former will then determine our view of that common initial condition, of which those traditional or so-called historical relations are, so to speak, only the points of the branches, or the extremities of the lines, which diverge from it as their common origin.

Thus we shall obtain pictures of a series of conditions which we could not discover from any historical tradition, and from which we must then contemplate the farther development, till we arrive at conditions which can be seized historically. The question here is to determine with all possible accuracy the degree, the species, and the peculiarity of the pre-historic conditions, and, as far as possible, to obtain a complete picture of them. Hitherto this has nowhere been attempted in a proper manner.* It would be but a short step, for example, to determine the condition of the people that once spoke the mother tongue of the Indo-Germans, or even,—a thing which

---

* This, of course, would have been differently stated, if it had been recently written.

would be much simpler—the character of this Indo-Germanic original idiom.*

If we thus succeed in placing before our minds a series of pre-historic conditions, the further task remains of penetrating backward again from these, and if any family relationship manifests itself as existing among them, to investigate the prior condition that lies at the basis of it. Thus a comparative view of the original relations of the Indo-Germanic and Semitic languages, and of the other members of the sexual family, must enable us to know the epoch which preceded its division into different branches. Yea, from the original condition of the sexual family we shall be able, with the aid of the other families of pronominal languages, to arrive at the fundamental type of this extensive family of languages. In this way, however, we must endeavor to examine the connection of all differently developed human relations, and where this connection manifests itself, to obtain the clearest possible ideas of the initial conditions. In this pursuit of the ramifications of the human race, some light may certainly be obtained at once by a mere comparison of those members which are distinguished by their faithful preservation of what is ancient. But any deeper and more accurate investigation must take into consideration all the offshoots of each of the groups under comparison that fall within our knowledge. For instance, Sanskrit, so-called Old Persian and Zend, Greek, Latin, Gothic, Lithuanian and Old Slavic, are certainly not sufficient to enable us to arrive at an exact comprehension of the original relations of the structure of the Indo-European tongues. The original Germanic form of speech, derived

* An attempt of this kind seems to have been made recently by A. Schleicher in his *Compendium of the Comparative Grammar of the Indo-Germanic Languages.* Weimar, Vol. I, 1861. II, 1862.

6

from the manifold variety of all the German dialects, must take the place of Gothic, and, in a similar manner, the other factors of what has hitherto passed as Indo-Germanic comparative grammar must be replaced, if the linguistic life of this race is to appear to us in its true light.

We have here intentionally spoken only of conditions which might be traced up to the same starting-point, not of peoples springing from one stem. For the relationship of different human conditions certainly does not stand in direct ratio to the blood-relationship of the peoples who represent them How much easier is it, for example, to trace the conditions of the Romance peoples outside of Italy to the condition of Rome, than to find drops of Roman blood in their veins! It is certainly not merely their tropical position that renders the Galla physically so similar to the negro, whilst his speech, which claims Semitic kinship, hardly manifests a proportionate influence of the *Bâ-ntu* element. Such a transition of conditions from one people to another is one of the most interesting spectacles in the history of human development; it is, besides, of extreme importance for that development. It has frequently contributed to advance its culture, inasmuch as in a certain way a fusion of different conditions takes place, or at least, in the contest between them, a reaction of the vanquished condition upon the stronger aggressive one. The influence, for example, of the Keltic upon the formation of the relations of the Romance peoples is still far from being sufficiently appreciated.

There is, therefore, certainly, a relation between the conditions of a people and the proportions of the different bloods that enter into their constitution. This relation is however by no means of such a nature as to confound

them, and hence science must hold the two as far asunder
as possible. The investigation of the physical affinities of
different nations belongs to natural research, whereas the
investigation of the various human conditions is the
province of universal philology.

The conditions of a people depend mainly upon their
mode of thought; this is the most important and influen-
tial condition. All others can be comprehended only
according to and in it. It is it that makes man man, and
it is only in the formation of it that humanity develops
itself. It is therefore the chief aim of philology to follow
the unfolding of thought in humanity, and the moulding
of it into different thought-forms. The development of
the other conditions of humanity will naturally follow,
and what cannot be traced back to the mode of thought
does not really belong to the sphere of philology.

We know the condition of a thing by its manifestations.
The manifestations of thought are various; but no one
of them is of more importance than language. For it is
through language and with language that man as a
thinking being has developed himself. It is communication by means of speech that brings his thinking to
greater clearness, by bringing the different modes of
thought into mutual furthering communication with each
other. By means of speech man is able to hold with
more tenacity the impressions already obtained, and thus
better to combine the old with those whose action is
fresher, and generally each one with every other, and to
work them up into intuitions. It is the spring of self-
consciousness, inasmuch as it is what enables man to
distinguish himself and his emotions from the external
world, and so to become conscious of both. Thus it is
only by means of it that true development of thought can
take place; for as Wilhelm von Humboldt's last letter to

Göthe clearly states: "Our entire possession of ideas is just what we, placed outside of ourselves, can cause to pass over into others."

When we thus know what language accomplishes, how it is the basis of our existence as human beings, and when, in the mode indicated, we can follow it through the different phases of its development, and are even able to obtain an image of the stages of its formation which lie nearest to its origin—still we do not thereby obtain any information as to the manner of its rise. Yet I consider this question as certainly a very important one, and do not look upon it as useless to enquire how that arose which lifted us above the animal world, and threw us into a path, whose goal, fortunately for us, we cannot espy.

A solution of this problem, however, is not impossible, for the reason that language is merely a product of that life-giving power of volition which we must recognize as the principle penetrating the other organisms.

The voluntary movement which our consciousness compels us to assume as an axiom in ourselves is a power which is certainly inexplicable from what we know of chemistry and physics, but is not the less a matter of fact on that account. This sort of force which we must regard as the foundation and basis of human existence, we are also obliged to recognize as the agent in animal existences, wherein we see it in the different stages of development. Seeing that we are thus able to bring into connection the quivering of the most undeveloped of the infusoria, with the action of thinking individuals, which is the result of consciousness, there is nothing authorizing us to make a separation between the latter and the general movement of the animal and vegetable cellular matter or protoplasm; this seems rather to manifest itself as its undeveloped appearance. It is indeed possible that the force which lies at the basis of voluntary movement would lose something of its inexplicability, if we were to follow its unfolding more accurately into detail, and, watching carefully every mode of its expression, to exhaust all the phases of its development from the lowest up to the most advanced. For what reason should we not examine more closely why in the plant it remains confined to the individual cell, whereas it grasps the whole of the animal organism, and in beings connected through language, effects more and more a harmonious interaction of individual volitions, and a combination into larger unities, such as the family, people, church, state, and other unions variously formed for various purposes.

However, the task of philology is merely the consideration of the products of volition in this last stage. But, if we try to gain an acquaintance with the development of any epoch, we can do this only by obtaining a picture of the conditions from which it started, and hence pursuing their further development through the given space of time.

But as all investigation of the course of human evolution, save in cases where it is handed down historically, is impossible, unless, starting from the lowest known condition, we ascend as it were to the higher; and, as the path of development that lies between the different cognizable conditions can be made out only by combination from those given magnitudes; so, likewise, we cannot arrive at a knowledge of the rise of humanity, the ascent of human nature from animal existence, save by a comparison of the lowest conditions of humanity with those of the highest formations in the animal world. We must examine and see what there is in animal nature analogous to that which is characteristic of man; from which of the faculties

of the former, human life could arise, under favorable
circumstances. For the fact that conditions similar to
those of humanity can no longer develop themselves from
animal speechlessness proves nothing, just as the fact
that the progress of a language like that of the Hottentots to the stage of development reached by its no very
distant Indo-Germanic relatives is now impossible, proves
nothing.

We must greatly lament in our inquiries that an investigation of those stages that preceded humanity has hitherto not been undertaken with the view to learn in how
far they contain germs for the development of human existence.† Were this done, we should learn to understand
in quite a different way the significance of the act of
humanization. We should also be able to obtain a much
more reliable and accurate picture of the course of it,
whereas, at present, we can attempt to depict it only in

---

* Those classes of animals that stand next to man, are, if not externally, at least internally, in a different condition from that in
which they were at the period when humanity arose. Being as yet
hardly formed, they were then not only more susceptible of change,
but there also lay in them a stronger impulse toward further progress
and the attainment of a higher stage. This impulse had to be satisfied, as was done in the case of human beings; or, if it remained
long without satisfaction, it would necessarily be extinguished, and
therewith ceased the possibility of their freeing themselves from the
condition in which they were. This condition became all the while
more and more confirmed, and what at first was the uncertain advance of a forward impulse toward formation, and, at the same time,
the first steps towards a further development of this power, forms
now the petrified, stereotyped forms of a species of animals, which
seems to have long ago been deprived of the possibility of internal
change.

† Interesting illustrations of this subject are to be found in Dr. G.
Jäger's Essay *On the Origin of Human Language* in the *Ausland*
for 1867; Nos. 42, 44, 47.

vague outlines. The question here is, to show how, by the method of comparing various conditions, results of no mean order are arrived at in respect even to their development, although these conditions are as dissimilar as those of human and those of animal nature, the latter being of course taken in their highest, the former in their lowest stages of development.

It will be best for us to begin by settling the difference between the word in human speech and the character of animal sounds—a difference which will at once be made evident by closer definition. In the lower animals generally, sound is only the expression of feeling; not indeed that the animal means thereby to communicate its feeling; but simply that there is connected with feelings, a certain peculiar activity of the organism, and by that a sound is produced. In the animal, sound has not yet become the line of demarcation between its own self and the object. It can however become so, and will become so more and more, in proportion as there is a tendency in it, to become the image of the external world. With the waking of this tendency, humanity existed; to satisfy it completely is humanity's unattainable goal. All that is intermediate is simply different stages and forms of its development. But in order that this tendency should manifest itself, it was in the first instance necessary that, in the creature producing the sound, there should arise the consciousness, not only of the sound as distinguished from the feeling that accompanied it, but also of the necessary connection between the two. How it was possible for this to take place, we will next consider.

Let us suppose a creature endowed with a very strong capacity for forming sounds, but with a tendency to imitation such as we find among the species of animals that stand next to man, it is not conceivable that a union of

the two faculties should fail to take place in it. Imitation
of sounds we find even among parrots; but their capacity
for imitation is of quite a different character from that of
the apes, which is limited to the imitation of creatures
similar to themselves—a limitation which we regard as
highly important.* In the imitative creature there is an
effort to assimilate itself as far as possible to creatures
of the same form, an effort which, in the animal world
accomplishes its aim in a merely external manner, whereas the internal accomplishment of it is possible, only
through language.

If, now, such a creature, whose nature it is to unite
particular states of feeling with vocal utterance, imitates
similar expressions of feeling coming from animals of its
own class, the sound which it thus produces is one to
which its organs are already accustomed. The particular
feeling, however, which was wont to occasion it, has not
produced it this time, but it owes its origin to the
tendency to imitation. But, as it was formerly called
forth by that feeling, it has become so much accustomed
to be accompanied by it, that the feeling is superinduced,
even when the sound is produced without its agency.
When, then, through this imitation, there sprang up a
consciousness of the sound, and its production was only
followed by the presence of the feeling, whereas, formerly, the sound was merely an involuntary accompani-
ment of the feeling—then it was that the sound came
into consciousness, distinguished from the feeling to which

*This limitation of the tendency of the ape to imitation depends
on the nature of the animal, in so far as it is manifested by gesticulation, and the external behavior of a dissimilar creature is naturally
insusceptible of imitation, or, at all events, does not naturally pro-
voke to imitation. The parrot, on the contrary, following its eye
and not its ear in imitation, can as readily reproduce the creaking of
a door as the cry of another bird.

it naturally belonged, and yet as having a necessary connection with it. The involuntary utterance of a feeling thus became a sign of a feeling. The rise of the consciousness of the difference between the sound and the feeling, this positing of the sound as a separate entity, which is transformed by the volition laying hold of it, into its instrument—is the first step in the process whereby man became man.*

To be sure the imitation of gestures may lead to results similar to those which imitation of sound here produces. But, on the one hand, the expression of feeling by gesticulation is too various and too changeable, to be readily seized and fixed with the same definiteness as sound. On the other hand, gesticulation affects the entire organism in such a way, that distinction between it and the feelings which call it forth would not take place so readily. Modulation of the voice is much easier for creatures endowed with the power of producing sound, as is shown by the perfection which song-birds display in distinguishing tones. For this reason a further development of sound-language is possible in quite another way than it could have been in the case of gesticulative language, if such had been developed instead of the other.†

But we do not mean to distinguish possibilities that are

*Whether, and to what extent such first attempts at language (i. e. the utterance of expressions of feeling not as such, but their voluntary application, in order to express the accompanying feeling, or the feeling presumed in their companions) are discoverable in the animal world, and why they have not developed these into a complete conventional language, deserves closer investigation.

†Could an unusually delicate, developed sense of touch be capable of giving rise to a language of touch, such as distinguished naturalists think they have discovered in ants and insects of that class?

7

not actual; let us suppose the word already existing with
the first elements of articulation. How did the further
development of language take place? And how did the
self-consciousness develop itself in and through its further
formation. Of course, self-consciousness must be confined to beings that have learnt to distinguish between
their feelings and the objects which call them forth. But
a clear distinction of this sort is possible only through
the articulated word, placing itself between them, and
thus its beginning coincides with that of self-consciousness, and thereby of humanity, of human existence. The
further history of the word therefore includes the formation of the self-consciousness, and therefore the career of
the development of human existence.

But the word, having arisen in all cases through imitation, and in intercourse with creatures of the same species,
is from its nature as a mere simple sound, of two-fold
origin. On the one hand, in certain movements of feeling,
it might come from the direct action of the organs; on
the other hand, the tendency to imitation in creatures
having the power of producing sound, would of necessity
be directed to those sounds which were most striking to
the ear. But both, not only the interjection, but also the
imitative sound are, in their nature, mere involuntary expressions of feeling; inasmuch as the play of the organs
which produces the sound, just as in the former case it is
excited by feeling, is in the latter excited by the equally
unconscious tendency to imitation. Therefore, in the
account given above of the manner in which the word
arose, I have been able to throw the two together without
any harm. For all that I have there said of the interjection may at once be asserted of the imitative sound. The
latter is accompanied by the feeling of the phenomenon
imitated, or of the representation aroused along with it

in the mind,* and may therefore be well included under
the term interjection.

The external form of the first words was of course
entirely similar to that of the interjections from which
they sprang,† and can therefore be arrived at only from a
consideration of the interjections that remain in our
languages, and of the so-called onomatopoetic words,
or words that imitate sounds, together with a comparison between them and the sounds of the animal
voice.

In this initial condition of language we cannot properly

[* The German word here is *Gemüth*, which has no English equiv-
alent. It comes pretty near the Greek word Θυμός, and means the
seat of the passions, feelings, and emotions. TR.]

† Although I cannot say that I am altogether satisfied with Humboldt's definition of articulate sound (Introduction to the work on the
Kawi Language, p. lxxxi.), yet it does not seem to me to belong to
the nature of articulate sound as such, that it should be a limited
sound having a definite form (K. Heyse, *System der Sprachlaute*,
1852, p. 5, et seq). I believe that, in its origin, and also in the first
stages of the development of language, the word does not differ
externally from the animal utterance of feeling. But the further
progress of the development of language renders it necessary that
the articulate sound should become more and more limited and
shaped. But this view of mine is in harmony with the statement on
page 7 of Heyse's above mentioned work : " It is articulated only to
the degree in which the mental import is internally articulated, that
is, logically divided and formed," although I should have expressed
even this thought somewhat differently. I should rather make the
two clauses exchange places. But this is due altogether to the view
which I hold of the relation of thought and speech, and which is
somewhat different from that of Heyse. According to him, language
is an efflux of thought. It seems to me that this view does not
give sufficient prominence to the fact that it is only through it that
man comes to consciousness, and that to a great extent, particularly
in the beginnings of human existence, the word gives birth to the
thought.

speak of a system of sounds or of a division of words
into their individual elements. Every word formed in
itself a united vocal whole, which certainly had not the
remotest resemblance to the simple elements to which
our etymologists imagine they can reduce the vocabulary
of languages. The different organs used in the production
of sound were certainly put in action in a manner much
more manifold, more energetic, and differing very consid-
erably from our method of producing sound.* Clicking

* The comparative science of language places beyond doubt, as
the direct result of observations made on the direction taken by the
development of a system of sounds, the fact that in general that
system of sounds is to be considered the most original which requires
the greatest amount of mechanical exertion for their enunciation.
The tendency in the vocal development of language is to make the
pronunciation as easy as possible. In this relation, we need only
refer to the manner in which English, the most advanced member of
the Germanic family of languages, is pronounced, as compared with
its nearest relatives. But nothing can be a greater mistake than, for
example, the idea that an apparent simplicity of phonology, such as
we find in the language of the Sandwich Islanders, is a proof of
original condition. A comparison with the other Polynesian dialects
proves, as an incontestable historically established fact, that the
unusual poverty of consonants in Hawaian is not original, and that the
more the cognate dialects have preserved a rich consonantal system,
the more the antiquated forms have been preserved in them. Among
all the languages with which I am acquainted, that of the South
African Bushmen (called by the Hottentots, Saan, by the Kaffirs,
Abatua, and in Setshuána, Baroa) far excels the rest in respect to
the strength of the mechanical exertion necessary for its pronunciation. A language like this, in which the majority of the words are
pronounced with one of the clicks (the number of different clicks
amounting at least to six), and several with very energetic gutturals,
must be made an object of special attention if we would arrive at
even an approximate idea of the original vocal elements from which
human language sprang. In this language, not only the tongue, as
in Hottentot, but also the lips click. It seems to me that our modern
systems of sounds might with as good reason be regarded as mere

offshoots, extremely weakened and softened down according to
definite laws, of such original phonologies, as the modern methods
of writing, particularly the stenographic, are considered to be de-
scendants of a hieroglyphic picture-writing transmogrified for
practical purposes. But in how far a system of sounds like that of
the Bushmen shows points of coincidence with sounds produced by
the apes resembling man, is a question which seems to me well
deserving of closer investigation. On this subject, the Jena professor
of zoölogy, Dr. Haeckel, writes to me (15th September, 1866) the
following : " The language of the apes has not hitherto received from
" zoölogists that attention which it deserves, and there do not exist
" any accurate descriptions of the sounds uttered by them. They
" are designated sometimes simply as howls, sometimes as cries, clicks,
" roars, &c. Remarkable clicking sounds, produced not only with
" the lips, but also, though seldomer, with the tongue, I have myself
" frequently heard in zoölogical gardens, and from apes of very
" different species, but I have been unable to find anywhere an
" account of them. Evidently these sounds have not interested
" most observers. Perhaps it will be interesting to you to learn that
" three years ago there appeared a work by the great English
" zoölogist, Huxley, and soon after another and more extensive one
" by the German, Carl Vogt, in which the evidence of the descent
" of the human race from the apes, founded on embryological and
" palæontological investigations, was stated with such pointedness,
" that no scientific zoölogist any longer has any doubt on the subject.
" Among all the hitherto discovered living species of men, the
" Australasian negroes in New Holland, and the Bushmen who are
" related to these in many ways, are the ones that stand nearest to
" the apes. Among the living known apes, the Anthropoides (the
" Gorilla and Engeco in Central Africa, and the Orang and Gibbon
" in India) are the ones most closely related to man, although they
" are by no means his progenitors, but lateral branches from common
" progenitors. The genealogy of the Primate Order would be
" somewhat like this (see plate). The common family group of the
" ape order, which is sprung from lower mammals, first divided into
" two principal branches, the thin-noses (Catarrhinæ) and the flat-
" noses (Platyrrhinæ), the former having thirty-two, the latter
" thirty-six teeth. The former inhabited exclusively the old world,
" Asia and Africa, the latter the new world, America. The thin-
" noses, or Catarrhinæ, the apes of the old world, remained for the
" most part with tails (Menocerca). One portion of them, however,

sounds, even perhaps the clapping of hands and other
sounds not produced with the organs of the mouth, as
they certainly served for the expression of feeling, must
also have been transformed from interjections into articulate words of the original language.

But, if we should measure these words belonging to
the earliest stage of humanity by the standard of our
syllables, we should certainly find that their duration was
not limited to that of one of our syllables. The nature
of the interjection would always depend entirely upon
the organs which were called into sounding activity by
the feeling which occasioned it. The product of this
activity would certainly only in rare cases be a simple
element, according to our grammatical analysis. By the
same simple feeling, the organs of sound might in suc-
cession be made to produce different utterances, and these,
although not really composite, would frequently bear
more analogy to our polysyllabic than to our monosyllabic
words. The idea that all languages must be reduced to
originally monosyllabic roots is a mistake—for this, if for
no other reason, that they contain a large number of
onomatopoetic words (e. g. *hai i* in *hai.fa.a* the Galla

"lost their tails, and developed themselves into forms resembling
"men, or into man-apes *(Anthropoides* or *Lipocerca)*. Of these we
"find still living the Gibbon *(Hylobates)* and the Orang *(Satyrus)*
"in Southern Asia, and the Chimpanzee *(Engeco)* and Gorilla *(Gina)*
"in Africa. From a now extinct branch of these Anthropoides was
"developed (probably in Southern Asia) the human race, which
"afterwards divided into 5–10 different species, the so-called races
"of men." Compare Haeckel, *General Morphology of Organisms*,
Vol. II, pp. cxli, and 423–432. Berlin, 1866; and Haeckel, *On the
Origin and Genealogy of the Human Race*, Berlin, 1868.

A passage in Du Chaillu's last work *(Travels in Ashango Land*,
English original edition, pp. 371, 372) seems to show that, at least
with a certain approximation, the sounds produced by the Chimpanzee
are not unlike the tones of human speech.

See page 54

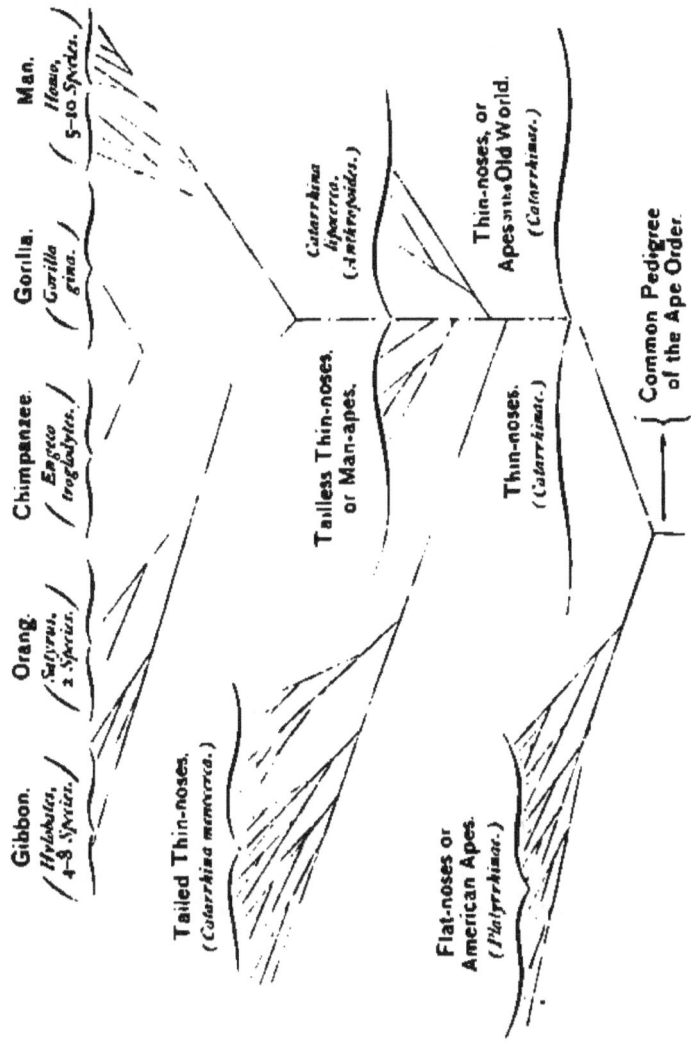

Man.
(*Homo,*
5-10 *Species.*)

Gorilla.
(*Gorilla*
gina.)

Chimpanzee.
(*Engeco*
troglodytes.)

Orang.
(*Satyrus,*
2 *Species.*)

Gibbon.
(*Hylobates,*
4-8 *Species.*)

Catarrhina
lipocerca.
(*Anthropoides.*)

Thin-noses, or
Apes of the Old World.
(*Catarrhinae.*)

Tailless Thin-noses.
or Man-apes.

Thin-noses.
(*Catarrhinae.*)

Tailed Thin-noses.
(*Catarrhina menocerca.*)

Flat-noses or
American Apes.
(*Platyrrhinae.*)

Common Pedigree
of the Ape Order.

Genealogical Tree of the Ape Order.

word for sneeze *) which cannot possibly be called mono-syllabic, although they owe their origin to simple imitation. Repetition of the same sound I have found in the first stage of language in very many (perhaps in most) words; yet this did not affect their simple character. The expression of feeling by sound is seldom limited to a single utterance, but is called forth oftener than once by the continuance of the feeling—in most cases several times, nay, very many times. To the first words, however, as mere copies or offspring of expressions of feeling, we must ascribe a character entirely corresponding to these; and what can be shown as true with regard to the external form of the latter, we may boldly ascribe to the former.

The meaning also of the individual word of the original language necessarily depended on the feeling which was associated with the interjection from which it sprung. But as this interjection did not owe its origin to a single object or condition, but was the product of an entire state of feeling (*Gemüth*), so also single objects or feelings could not have been designated by the first words. They, the words of the original language, were to the consciousness mere expressions of states, arising from a complex of different feelings working together. The same state, or at least similar ones readily convertible with it in the consciousness, might, however, be occasioned in mani-fold ways by the most diverse objects. The difference in the producing causes, so long as the effect was the same, would not be felt in the first period of man's progress towards consciousness; but all further develop-

---

* The clicks / (dental) and! (palatal) here represent the characters *t* and *d* of the Tutschek alphabet, to which, to judge of the descrip-tion of it, they seem to correspond. Lepsius, however, represents the Tutschek *t̠* by *t̤*, and its *d̠* by *g'*.

ment necessarily urged him on to distinguish his individual
feelings, and to obtain from them an intuition of the
objects and conditions which produced them.

But as I was able with reason to affirm that, as the sound
expressive of feeling gives us information of the life of
feeling, so the word gives us information of the consciousness of feeling; in like manner, I must affirm that the
relation between consciousness and language is very
different from that which subsists between the interjection
and the feeling. For the feeling expresses itself in sound
only in exceptional cases; so that, of the whole of the
sensuous life of any creature however largely endowed
it may be with the power of producing sound, nothing
beyond a very few fragments is manifested by its voice.
Sound is a mere accidental accessory to feeling. Not only
is there feeling without it, but it is comparatively seldom
that feeling is made perceptible to the ear. Consciousness, on the other hand, awoke in man with the birth of
the first words; its character was shaped entirely by their
signification, and its extent is not greater than the sum of
what is expressed by words. Speech and consciousness
are not thinkable apart; the one could not possibly have
arisen save along with the other, and through the rise of
the other; thus the one is the exact image of the other.
The further development of self-consciousness took place
necessarily only along with and because of the development of language. What has really passed clearly into
the consciousness must be produced through language and
be visible in it. The language of a people is always a
copy of the thoughts that have come into its consciousness.

How limited must have been the condition of the
consciousness in the initial period of humanity! Consciousness of states of feeling was all that could then have

been awake in man; consciousness, too, only of such states as had been accompanied with sounds that in the way above described had become words. But since, as we have said, it was only the smallest portion of the sensuous life that expressed itself in sound, and since the whole of these sounds expressive of feeling could hardly have passed into words, we can hardly imagine how little of that which was felt passed into the consciousness, and how vague even that little must have been. There existed as yet but a mere prelude to cognition.

But in order to make any real progress in this direction, language and the consciousness united and bound up with it had to be further formed. The meaning of the individual words was rendered more limited by the production of new words, either from interjections or imitative sounds. But the consciousness passed into a new stage, from which a true progress in development was possible only when the material of language was able in itself by reciprocal action to produce new elements.

With this further unfolding of the formative process of language begins the second stage in the awakening of human cognition from an animal-like state of unconsciousness. But in order to arrive at this, we must try to make ourselves thoroughly acquainted with the character of speech in the first stage. In it, intercourse through speech consisted simply in this, that when one was visited by a particular state of feeling for which he knew a word, and wished to communicate this feeling to another, he uttered that word. But, inasmuch as this word was entirely similar to the interjection from which it had sprung, this condition of vocal utterance was not distinguished from the speechless one that preceded it by anything save the consciousness, which in this case was instrumental in the production of the sound.

8

Again, however, it was possible that there should be
states of feeling which reminded the one who wished to
attempt to express them of two others, which already
had got words to designate them. There was nothing
more natural than that, in order to express them, he should
put the two words together. This was the second stage,
and in it the basis was first laid for the separation between
the outward manifestations of the conscious and unconscious expression of feeling.

In the third and last stage of the first period, before
this separation had fully taken effect, there had already
in this way, by the union of known words, been formed
expressions for a number of states of feeling which, being
formerly accompanied by no sounds, had therefore in the
previous stages not been expressible by words, and a
consciousness of which had not yet been attained. This
however took place in a manner peculiar and differing
essentially from the previous one. As feelings were now
expressed by several words, they appeared to the consciousness as made up of the states designated by these
words, notwithstanding that they might be really much
more simple than the elements of which they seemed to
be composed.

But, if they were so (that is to say, more simple), and
in proportion as they were so, the more readily would the
feeling of the connection between the two combined
words necessarily impress itself on the soul. In use, they
would necessarily grow together more and more closely,
whereas others were held more loosely apart. Next, to
unite words combined in a conception as far as possible
into a whole in sound was a very natural effort of the
linguistic tendency. But sounds brought closely together
could not continue without mutual influence. Changes
of sound accommodated them to each other; and thus two

words that were formerly distinct readily passed over into
a new one, which did not, either in form or concept,
indicate what its elements had been. This process would
necessarily be facilitated in cases where the sounds out
of whose fusion the new word had arisen had already
ceased to be used as simple words, and out of composition.

Thus the second period in the career of the development of language begins with the external separation
between it and the unconscious expressions of animal
sensuous life. It is not till this point that language can
be regarded as a secure possession, inasmuch as the
previous absence of distinction between the form of words
and that of sounds expressive of feeling still made it
seem possible that their internal distinction, which was
seized and established by the will only, should vanish, and
humanity sink back into the state of unconsciousness.

The distinction between sound and feeling could not
arise in the consciousness until the sound came to be not
so much the result of a feeling as of a combination which,
so to speak, forcibly united it to the feeling which it was
to express. The fact that it was not spontaneously produced by the organs when affected by a particular state
of feeling, but was entirely independent of the action of
affection in the organism—nay, perhaps even opposed to
it—was naturally of the greatest importance in holding
asunder the feeling and the expression of the feeling in
the consciousness.

The distinction between feeling and expression of feeling, however, necessarily preceded the separation between
the object and the feeling occasioned by the object.
Intuition of objects developed itself only from intuition
of the feelings called forth by them.

Confusion of concepts could be diminished only by their
progressive limitation. A word that expressed a state of

feeling very generally and indefinitely was limited by the addition of another to a part of the meaning inherent in it. So long as the compound character of the word was still perceptible this particular feeling appeared in the consciousness only as a combined one. When the appearance of composition afterwards vanished from the word and it appeared to the ear as a simple sound, the concept designated by it was seized by the consciousness as a simple one. But while the concepts, which at first were so much confused, were thus sundered, the things which gave occasion to the feeling, i. e. objects and their conditions, came nearer to the consciousness; although in this period no real conscious intuition was reached, that indeed being something which can be arrived at only when a distinction is made between these.

However, before we can pass to the manner in which the consciousness was awakened by the duplicity of the provocatives of feeling, we must give more special attention to many phenomena which occur in the second period. We have not yet touched upon the case in which only one part of a compound word had ceased to be used as a simple word. When this took place, the new word would evidently, and of necessity, appear as a modification of the other element which was still protected in its isolated signification.

Thus, by the new process of derivation, it became possible to call different shades of an already existing concept into consciousness, and, on the analogy of the derivative words already formed, further divisions of fundamental concepts could be effected by means of such sounds as had ceased to have any value in and for themselves, receiving their value only from combination with others.

Thus, a word in the second period might have ten different origins. Either:

A. It corresponded, without any addition, to the interjection from which it arose, *Simple*, 1.

Or,

B. It was composed of two such simple words, or two simple word factors, whereof

   a. Both still occur as separate words; *Compound*, 2.

   b. The first element still occurs as a separate word.

      α. The second, however, only in compounds. *Derived with Suffix*, 3.

      β. The second does not occur elsewhere at all. *Strengthened at the end*, 4.

   c. The second element still occurs as a separate word.

      γ. But the first only in compounds. *Derived with prefix*, 5.

      δ. The first does not occur elsewhere. *Strengthened at the beginning*, 6.

   d. Neither part is any more used by itself.

      ε. Yet both are still found in compounds. *Concreted*, 7.

      ζ. The first still occurs in compounds; the second not. *Inflected at the end*, 8.

      η. The second still occurs in compounds; the first not. *Inflected at the beginning*, 9.

      θ. Neither occurs elsewhere. *Fused*, 10.

The course which was taken in the development of words is best shown by the following table:

1st Stage	Simple word [Interjection] (1)		Simple word [Interjection]
2d Stage	Compound word (2)		
3d Stage	Derived with suffix (3.)		Derived with prefix (5.)
4th Stage	Strengthened at the end (4.)	Concreted (7)	Strengthened at the beginning (6.)
5th Stage	Inflected at the end (8.)		Inflected at the beginning (9.)
6th Stage	Fused (10.)		

With letters, the preceding table will take the following
shape:

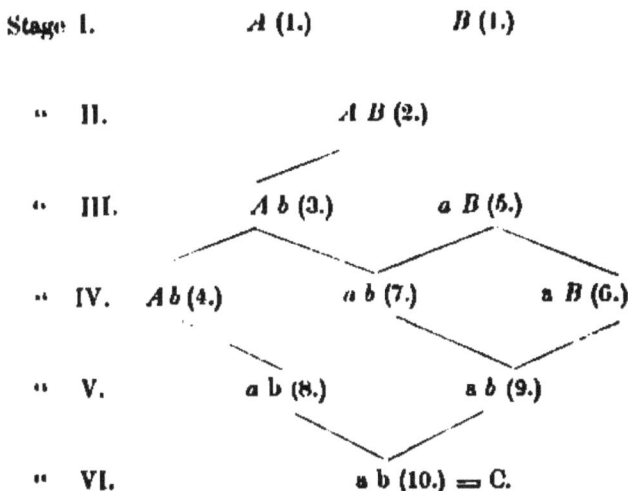

Stage I.   *A* (1.)   *B* (1.)

"   II.   *A B* (2.)

"   III.   *A b* (3.)   *a B* (5.)

"   IV.   *A b* (4.)   *a b* (7.)   *a B* (6.)

"   V.   *a b* (8.)   *a b* (9.)

"   VI.   *a b* (10.) = C.

A fused word appears naturally to the feeling as a
simple one again; and while in this way new simple
elements continue to be obtained, which have not been
interjections, but have been separated from them by
several stages of development in respect not only of their
form but also of their signification, there was developed
more and more a self-consciousness distinct from the
immediate sensuous life.

Moreover, since we have here made reference only to
words made up of one or two elements, it is plain (since
there is nothing to prevent more than two from being
combined) that the multiplicity of the different modes of
forming words might be much greater still in the second
period, especially when we take into consideration further
that changes of sound more or less important might affect

sometimes the one element, sometimes the other, sometimes several, or even all at once. Words formed in these different ways would of necessity excite the consciousness differently, as is clear especially from what we have already said of the difference between the modes in which single, compound, and fused words are apprehended.

Thus far, we have sketched the course of linguistic development as if it had been one which advanced steadily in one direction. But in truth there were, even in its first stages, two modes of formation possible. The individual elements, instead of being fused together, might be held rigidly asunder. A departure from the form of the interjection lying at the basis of the word might likewise be effected in such a case by a change of sound arising from a striving after the easiest possible pronunciation.

That languages did develop themselves one-sidedly in this direction must be admitted. The only question is whether there are any such languages in existence now. In regard to the idioms of Further Asia, I would not yet positively assert that even in the first period of their development they adhered to the principle of holding the words asunder in this way. Whether this principle did not obtain currency later, and whether they did not accompany the rest for a considerable distance into the second period, must be shown by thorough-going comparative studies.[*] These would have to discuss particularly the question how a system of sounds has been developed in those languages, and in how far they possess such a system. For a language might have succeeded in forming a vocal

---

[*] I allow intentionally the whole of this to stand as it was written in the year 1853, because an examination of R. Lepsius' rigorous investigations as published in his able treatise on the *Phonology of Chinese and Thibetan, &c.*, Berlin, 1861, would here lead me too far away from my subject.

system, that is, in acquiring a few sounds, of which the mass of the different words seemed to be but combinations, by the formative process of the second period. The combination of the same sound with various others would alone give occasion to the recurrence of the same elemental word. The tendency to ease of pronunciation would however lead to the disappearance of those sounds which, from their rare occurrence, were unusual, or to fusion with others which were more usual. Vocal changes did something more. It would of course be only the later moments that could have any influence upon the formation of a vocal system in a language in which individual sounds did not come into any close contact.

But what appearance the earliest systems of sound presented we may well refrain from attempting to conjecture here. In any case, they were removed as far as possible from the pattern of Sanskrit or similar languages. The latter belongs to much later periods of language.

With the rise of the word, in so far as entirely distinct in sound and sense from the interjection, the question with regard to the origin of language is really settled, and the pursuit of the further development of the vocal form and conceptual import must be left to the history of language. In conclusion, I will now take a rapid and summary glance at my view of the mode in which the word arose.

The first phase of the existence of the word as such occurred when the sound expressive of a feeling was uttered, not as such, but was voluntarily employed for the purpose of calling up the accompanying feeling, or the corresponding one which was presumed to be felt by a companion.

In the second phase, the sound becomes fixed by usage as the conventional medium for the feeling which it indicates, and inasmuch as it is distinguished from the latter in the feeling and in the consciousness, it departs farther and farther from being an index of it, and soon becomes, even in form, a mere indication of the interjection to which it originally owed its origin, and with which in the beginning it was identical.

In spite of this, although in form and signification differing from the interjection and the feeling expressed by it, the word, both in form and import, leaned too much to the sensual world and the expression of it, and owed its origin to it too directly to be able as yet to embrace a clear independent concept.

Each word still designated an idea, standing for itself and modified only by itself, and formed, as we should say, an independent sentence.

Now it could not but happen that the desire should be felt to express feelings which were not in any very decidedly close relation to one particular feeling expressed by a complex of sound, but seemed to lie at once equally near to two such complexes. In this case, the most obvious thing was to put one of these after the other. This marks the beginning of the third phase.

Of two words thus unitedly expressing an idea, the one would of course usually appear in the consciousness as more necessary than the other for the concept expressed by both. Thus, even at an early period, a kind of distinction asserted itself in the consciousness between the principal and the subordinate part, between the word to be determined and the word which served to determine another.

In the first stages of the course of linguistic development I have endeavored to show how it is only with the rise and progress of language that man arrives at consciousness, and that no cognition can come into his consciousness otherwise than in and through language.

9

It is evident that clearness of consciousness must
increase in proportion as the external forms of speech
facilitate logical thinking. But they can do this only in
so far as that which is distinguished by them agrees with
the distinctions which urge themselves upon our cognition
as the most essential.

Our present thinking consists in a putting together of concepts whose images are awakened in us; and in like manner,
our speaking is a combining of individual words. The concepts which we have, however, are mere abstractions; they
are the result of the friction of the different feelings.

When I say, or what is really the same thing, think,
(for I think to exactly the same extent as I can speak) *the
horse in my stable is brown*, I put together mere abstractions
in order to designate the concept to be expressed. I
never saw brownness, or existence, or mine, or stable,
but I have seen millions of brown things, thousands of individual horses, many stables, have often thought of things
which belong to me, and am continually observing things
that are, that exist; I am surrounded by beings and am
one myself. (Dr. F. Leiber, in Schoolcraft's *Information
respecting the History, Condition and Prospects of the Indian
Tribes of the United States, Part II, p. 346.*)

But how do we pass from the mere consciousness of a
state of feeling with which human existence began to
these abstract concepts, and how did the word develop
itself from being the mere sign of a feeling into being
the basis of these concepts? The latter question, in our
view, comes first, and from the solution of it naturally
follows that of the other.

How the combination of concepts, which is effected by
the composition and consequent fusion of words must
lead more and more to abstractness and to a sundering of
them from individual feeling as the result of manifold

combinations, we have remarked above. But this, of and
by itself, did not lead to a division of the concepts into
classes. In the primitive words, the parts of speech were
entirely undistinguished. Even in cases where one of the
original elements did not suffice, in the already advanced
stages of linguistic development, to complete an expression, and several words had to be united into a sentence in
order to manifest a thought, we cannot speak of a real
distinction between the parts of speech.

The same word, without alteration, included a substan-
tival or a verbal concept, and could be used after the
manner of our adjectives, adverbs, &c. Thus, for example,
the perception of which one is conscious in hearing a
sound was designated by a word which arose from the
imitation of the sound. This perception was not at all
of an abstract or general character, but an altogether
concrete and individual one. For instance, had a word
been formed from imitation of the note of the cuckoo, its
concept could not possibly have been limited to that of
the bird, or to that of crying, or to any property of the
animal or its utterance, etc. etc.; but the whole situation,
in so far as it came into the consciousness, was indicated
by the word. The frequent hearing of the same sound
was of itself enough to bring the salient points of the
situation into consciousness; but the signification of the
word still comprehended the most heterogenous elements
whereof one was made more prominent in one connection,
another in another. But while in this manner, perhaps in
connection with a word indicating flying, the word cuckoo
made the concept of bird prominent, and the whole
designated the flying of the cuckoo, and while in another
connection the same word gave prominence to a property
or action of the cuckoo, this differed infinitely from the
principle which prevails in modern English, that a word

without any change may often belong to different parts of
speech. For, in English, the parts of speech, though not
always differing in sound, are always accurately distinguished in concept; while in the other case there was,
as yet, no consciousness of any difference, inasmuch as
neither form nor position had called attention to anything
of the kind.

For forms had not yet made their appearance, and
determinate position—as for example, in Chinese—could
prevail only in a language of very advanced internal
formation: we can think, even although the gradually
disappearing forms (as in English) which first called
attention to the distinction, have not been replaced. For
the parts of speech were certainly distinguished at an
early period by a vague feeling, and this even might have
contributed to establish a fixed order, which again would
of necessity give rise to a somewhat clear consciousness
of their difference.

Then there were combined with whole series of words
certain particles or derivative syllables, which became the
distinctive marks of their conceptual determination, indicating time, action, and particularly persons, or pointing to
the relation of concepts to the speaker (articles) or the like.

The origin of such formative elements in language will
be explained, if we keep in view the above described
processes whereby words are formed (pp. 59–64) somewhat
as follows: As a part of a word might disappear from use
as a separate word, so the same thing was possible in the
case of a part of a sentence—that is to say, it might
cease, when uttered by itself, to designate a concept, and
to have a meaning only in connection with others. Such
words, or as they are technically called, particles, belonged
both to the fusive and the isolative languages; they were
even rather more frequent in the latter than in the former.

With the appearance of them, and, in the fusive languages, with that of the derivative syllables, a consciousness of the form of the concept would necessarily manifest itself, since in this way, words or syllables which expressed merely the form of the concept individually, or as combined into a proposition, stood in a kind of opposition to the other more significant ones. The sort of form that came into use depended of course at first upon chance; but the more language developed itself, the more would formative words, or forms of words facilitating the aims of the understanding, necessarily come into use.

Thus was it found possible to pave the way for a distinction in form, and hence also in concept, between the parts of speech. But, even where it exists, it will hardly ever be completely realized. In particular cases, the words will lack the distinctive particles; in others the particles belonging to one part of speech are capable of being applied to another; and thus, even in numerous cases where it is not impossible to make the distinction, the consciousness of difference is not made clearly prominent by any close distinction between the parts of speech.

We do not find them completely distinguished till we come to the pronominal languages; although even in them different stages of progress are observable. This distinction is very closely connected with pronominal formation, and with the use of the pronouns and the union and fusion with other parts of speech.

But a consideration of the nature of pronouns and of the great significance of their influence upon the whole of the development of language would carry us too far into a region of the history of language which, although doubtless extremely interesting in itself, would be out of place in a treatise whose aim is merely to consider the origin of language.

TRANSLATOR'S NOTE.

Dr. Haeckel, to whom I wrote in regard to the publication of this translation, has sent me a very kind letter, from which I translate the following passage:

"JENA, March 31st, 1869.

"*Respected Sir:*

"Your kind letter which reached me yesterday, informing me that you had translated my cousin Bleek's essay ON THE ORIGIN OF LANGUAGE into English, gives me much pleasure. The essay has received much praise in Germany, and I hope it will have the same powerful effect in America also."

THOMAS DAVIDSON.

ST. LOUIS, May, 1869.

www.ingramcontent.com/pod-product-compliance
Lightning Source LLC
Chambersburg PA
CBHW020250090426
42735CB00010B/1869